Narad

Recent Poems

Recent Poems
Copyright : Prisma, Auroville
Author : Narad

First edition 2023

ISBN 978-93-95460-61-3 (Paperpack)
ISBN 978-93-95460-98-9 (ebook)

BISAC Code:
POE000000, POETRY / General
POE009000, POETRY / Asian / General
POE003000, POETRY / Subjects & Themes / Inspirational & Religious

Thema Subject Category:
DC, Poetry
DCF, Poetry by individual poets
D, Biography, Literature and Literary studies
DSC, Literary studies: poetry and poets

Cataloging-in-Publication Data for this title is available from the Library of Congress.

Published by:
PRISMA, an imprint of Digital Media Initiatives
PRISMA, Aurelec / Prayogshala,
Auroville 605101, Tamil Nadu, India

To Sri Aurobindo my eternal gratitude
for all He has given me and
all he has done for me.

INTRODUCTION

In these recent years, especially in Auroville and the last days of my life in America, I have been granted the blessing of poems descending en masse, often writing many a day. I cannot assess the quality but certainly they came without difficulty, and as they descended I expressed my gratitude to Sri Aurobindo, who has helped so many to write poetry. I leave it to those of greater knowledge to determine whether there is any value in them.

Contents

1. Among the Offering of Flowers — 9
2. A Poem for Aishwarya on Her Birthday There is a Beauty — 10
3. An American Indian Sonnet — 11
4. Casting Out Demons — 12
5. Collaborate with Truth — 13
6. Constant Seeking — 15
7. Falling Leaves — 16
8. God our Guide — 17
9. Homage to the Rose — 18
10. How to Express One's Gratitude? — 19
11. In America — 20
12. In Harmony with Human Hearts — 21
13. In Years Gone By — 22
14. Nature's Gold — 23
15. Branch of Time — 24
16. On the Death of a Friend — 25
17. She Died — 26
18. Snowflakes — 28
19. The Promised Goal — 29
20. The Wind — 30
21. The Wintry Soul of Man — 31
22. There Is an OM — 32
23. To Serve Both God and Man — 33

24. Uninvited Entities	35
25. Yagna Shastri	36
26. In Savitri	37
27. In the Home of the Gods	38
28. Melodies of Love	39
29. Moments	40
30. My Love for Thee	41
31. New and Glorious Home	42
32. On the Shore of Bengal's Sea	43
33. Preparing for Sleep	44
34. She Resides in Me	45
35. Sing Her Praise	46
36. The Errors of the Past	47
37. The Godhead's Face	48
38. The Grace Divine Shall Not Fail	49
39. The Mother's Kiss	50
40. The Psychic Being Grows	51
41. The Solace that is Rare	52
42. The Spirit's Upward Course	53
43. The Supermind	54
44. The Vaunted Calm	55
45. The World in Darkness	56
46. Their Clarion Call	57
47. This Body Old Yet Young	58
48. Towards Sri Krishna's Call	59
49. Your Longing Soul	60
50. Rosemarie	61

Among the Offering of Flowers

Let all be honest and admit
We let the hostile forces in
They come with scintillating wit
Inviting us to share their sin.

And though we hold in sanctity
In our secret heart the rose
Their darkness of such profundity
Holds us to their congress close.

And then we pray for Her relief
From evil beings entering
Trying to shake from us belief
With their nearly fatal sting.

We breathe again in restful hours
The atmosphere of calm and peace
Among the offering of flowers
And find in Love our soul's release.

A Poem for Aishwarya on Her Birthday
There is a Beauty

There is a beauty that cannot be seen
By the myopic vision of the eye.
It is a vision that has ever been
Descended from the heavens with a sigh
Of longing for the planes from which it came
And yet aware that earth is its true home,
A beauty so divine it has no name
But visible to those where Light has come
Into the soul and love is known divine,
In every stone, in every open flower,
It is the seeing of beauty as the sign
Of divinity: I hold you in that hour.

March 9, 2022

An American Indian Sonnet

Land of my body but not of my soul
My heart is here among the morning skies
But India holds me close, the inner call
Resounding as the heart within me cries.
Despite the Covid threats I must return
And lean on the Samadhi's sacred stone.
There is a fire within that once did burn
In days of silence when I lived alone
In beauty, music and the gardens fair,
Where I offered homage to the one above
Who holds me gently in her tender care
And pours on me the Grace of heaven's love.
One day I shall return to my true home
And hear His voice who softly whispers, "Come".

Casting Out Demons

The world today is overrun
With evil and its profligate hate
And yet the hour has begun
Of Good towards which we gravitate.

We will survive the Hostile's game
Create Truth's river and in its flow
Repeat unto the sea Her name
For surely through Her we shall know

And the mass of men shall feel Her love
And songs to Her shall come in strains
Of beauty descending from worlds above
And peace this troubled world attain.

Collaborate with Truth

Allow me to address in reverence
The Lord who stands above creation's field
And yet as in the stone has placed Himself
In flower, beast, in woman and in man.
He blossoms in the flower, in the fruit,
We cannot breath without His breath in us
We cannot move unless He moves our limbs.
In sleep he enters in and cradles our souls
That we may wake to morning with the glow
Of vibrant life pulsating through our hearts
Determined not to waste ourselves in thought
Of past remembrances but learn to live
The present full and in the future's dreams
Realize the gifts he gives and more
The future's dreams of immortality
That beckon us to tread His yoga's path,
Aware at every step Her Force ordains
Each upward thrust of being to the Light.
For She, Creatrix, mother of all lives
Carries us if we allow, to heights
Unreached in evolution's toil
And Nature's slow and steady steps ahead.

We stand now at the apex of a world
When earth abused, defoliate and worse,
Assaulted by the forces of the dark
Awaits the hour of the saving Grace
To heal her suppurating wounds and force
To flee from her the demons of the dark
Intent to govern the sentient light of life
That now on earth's horizons brightly dawns.
There is a Will, a conscious Force protects
Against destruction and the reign of death,
It asks us but to rise above ourselves
And in its peace collaborate with Truth.

Constant Seeking

This constant seeking for a light already ours,
A light we clothe with darkness of the mind
Or close behind the vital's darkened doors,
Seeking, seeking nowhere yet to find

The freedom from our poor selves desires.
The psychic being silently awaits
The opening, the greater self inquires
And yet the errant being hesitates.

Not fearing but inured in daily trials
Preferring not to challenge unkind chance
And bare the spirit to the outer wilds
And the human body give to circumstance.

Yet how shall God who silently dwells within
Reveal the Beauty, embracing us as kin?

Falling Leaves

Falling leaves like butterflies descend
Drifting through this air of mystery
And I aware of every season's end
In peace prepare to venture across the sea

To greet the home that always welcomes me,
Where sacred souls of the world come to meet
Partaking of a silent unity
And reverently bow before Her feet.

The road is long and the battle hard
For those who would dare to tread the upward way
Yet knowing that the goal is living God
They concentrate and meditate and pray.

And yet He is within the fragile frame
Originer and player of His game.

God our Guide

To heights supernal we must rise
All outworn vestiges discard
And with the aid of diviner eyes
Seek the way, though it be hard,

Though change came slowly in the past
When all the world in darkness wept
And a fleeting peace could not last
Few were those the Secret kept

Of transformation of the cells
That bodies might live eternally
As the anthem of a new life swells
To live in Truth immortally.

Now we our destiny decide
With God our anchor and our Guide.

Homage to the Rose

It is the hour when roses bloom
Abundantly in skies of rain
Or sun drenched knowing not of gloom
They sing of love and love's refrain

Touch open hearts with childlike glee
Their scented beauty on the air
Colours of antiquity
Perfection's shape beyond compare.

If we could offer like the rose
Our self of beauty to the One
We cherish at the daylight's close
Our journey into Light begun.

O world thy beauty blesses me
And washes over every soul
This divine creation mystically
Beckons us towards the goal.

How to Express One's Gratitude?

How to express one's ultimate gratitude
At seeing beauty never known before?
The storm has come and all the trees are nude
Yet camellias flower just outside my door
And all the world is touched with loving grace.
With two companions ever at my side,
In front of me the Mother's loving face
In His compassion does my soul abide.

The lake moves swiftly gilded with the light
And I in solitude awake to day,
No more the dark intrusion of the night
As now in peace I bow to Them and pray.
No other journey would I undertake
But here in earthly fragrance is my home
Though not to linger or the effort slake
Or in the pastures of desire roam
But cleave to Truth the beacon of our way
And certitude from which we shall not stray.

In America

In America the forces of evil toil
Relentlessly to uphold darkness' claim
Bring anarchy upon our blessed soil,
For domination is their single aim.

They would enslave the masses and revive
The power of the wanton Nazi state
And few who speak the truth would scarce survive
The brutal acts their minions would create.

Election is but one swift term away
Be careful world with whom you wish to choose
For choosing wrong will set the wheels in sway
For demonic control and surely we will lose

The freedom we once gained through heroes blood
And lose mankind's accumulated good.

In Harmony with Human Hearts

Sometimes I feel divorced from life
And live in Mother's Garden fair
Away from all this earthly strife
Yet know that I am needed there

To fix collective harmony
First within the being's core,
Build an elasticity,
Calm and peace and something more,

A stoic will to face the foe
Residing in our unseen parts
To let the healing Presence flow
In harmony with human hearts.

In Years Gone By

Once in many years gone by I read
In 'Savitri', the secret of the world
Evolving now at superhuman speed,
"To feel the eternal's touch in time-made things,"
This line is now amended and it reads,
Through all the many revisions by the Lord,
"To fix the eternal's touch in time-made things,".
Perhaps this is His last and ultimate draft
Accepted without question by the few
Or those who feel this is His greatest gift.
For me both 'feel' and 'fix' are divinely chosen
Words that I will cherish through lives to come.

Nature's Gold

It seemed so desolate a time of year
When all the greening of this vibrant life,
As leaves and flowers swift to disappear
In an instant gone by death's relentless knife.

Yet Spring in open hearts arrives again
And showers the soul with beauty and with bliss
The locked and frozen minds of mortal men
Astounded are touched by an eternal kiss.

And we who seek to make the world anew
Must face the first inevitable change
Within, this daunting trek that only few
Can climb above the mountain's awesome range,

Release the hidden founts of Nature's gold
Hidden from those who sadly have grown old.

December 7, 2020

Branch of Time

Leaning on a branch of time
I watch the world go floating by
What is man's most malignant crime,
Inertia with animosity.

There's greed too, corrupting all
And wealth the burden of the great,
Powerful yet doomed to fall
Knowing not the hour is late.

Change is upon us and change we must
Or hedonistic die incomplete
An animal nature with seething lust
Go down to death in defeat.

On the Death of a Friend

The late chrysanthemums that speak of life
Are budding now as I prepare to leave.
I read today that my dear friend had died,
His soul has flown – there is no cause to grieve
His gifts will live beyond the body's fall
For he instilled in youth the joy to know,
His body of books remain to enrich us all.
There is no death that has ultimately prevailed.
These master-souls return to earth again
In bodies new, in forms so lightly veiled
They labour to bring the living word to men
And work to end our enmity and strife.

She Died

She died but it was not a lonely death
I sat by her while blessed angels prayed
And I could hear the slowing of her breath
And the sweetness of her voice within me stayed.

She came to me a vision from the stars
And tended me when I fell gravely ill
Nothing in my distant memory mars
The beauty and the strength of her vast will.

To live for love and live to make her life
An offering to One whom she had seen
In India, the Mother, though the strife
Of poverty, detritus and the mean

Existence of the poor, the hapless mass
For whom a grain of rice was wealth enough
When it through drainage pipes would slowly pass,
Indigents, untouchables whose rough

Passage through life was like a blade
Driven into the heart of one so young,
And yet throughout her life her soul obeyed.
She moved to Auroville where enmity stung

Her soul and once again returning home,
Devoted worker, child of beauty and love
Her life's devotion one could swiftly sum,
A heavenly being descended from above.

Snowflakes

The snowflakes and their patterning on glass
In this life I may never see again
But they shall live, beauty shall not pass
And seeker of the truth I shall remain.

Far is the path on which our souls must go
But our beloved friend will take us there
Giving us the inner strength to know
That he, the Lord, the Generous, the Fair,

Has built his house in our transient abode.
In all past lives, he the charioteer
Has carried us across the challenging road
Informing us with strength that we not fear

The journey of the soul to endless light.
Over the windswept plains, the ocean's surge
To the future of the beautiful, the bright,
To that to which our silent souls doth urge

This frail time cart that ambles towards the One
To venerate all, the transformation begun.

The Promised Goal

When will I be purified
And live for Her in peace, content
To serve Him as my lord and guide
When all the angst in me is spent.

Struggle and strife are not the way,
Surrender truly is the key
Acknowledge the Mother's infinite play
And rest in the Divinity.

Many seasons, endless days
Have passed in useless wanderings
In which the vital nature plays
And spirit feels the painful stings

Of separation from the source.
Mother divine help this soul
To be set right and stay the course
That I may reach the promised goal.

The Wind

The wind, my friend, speaks to me
In sibilant whispers or in gusts
A furnace from eternity,
In all its moods and vehement lusts.

It comes a zephyr or a storm
Pelting the Garden with its hail
In springtime keeps the body warm
Or slashing like a banshee's wail

Scythes the flowers in their summer dress
Yet brings to earth the gentle rain
Or violent creates distress
Then laughing soothes us once again!

The Wintry Soul of Man

Harsh the wintry soul of man
Lagging in this hour of need
Obstinate since Time began
To grow as grows the tree from seed.

But human growth is cyclical,
No soul on earth can swiftly rise,
Progress is antithetical
When the ego-self seems the all-wise.

A sudden light upon the earth
A Grace unknown in times before,
The promise of supernal birth
Guiding man to open more

Is upon us now the day has come
To light our way and bring us home.

There Is an OM

There is an OM, the Word, Eternal Sound,
Creator of this world and worlds to be.
We sing the Name from every sacred ground
Anoint the valleys and earth in humility.

The flowers chant OM in their blossomings
The birds obeisance to OM is lent in song
We call OM down in all our offerings
For its transforming force we ever long.

Om Sri Aurobindo, grant our prayer,
Deliver us from all inconstancy
Transform all lives, the hapless and the fair,
Let us become the Image built by Thee.

To Serve Both God and Man

In the early stirring fields of youth
I walked alone and lonely was my way
Within my soul there was a search for Truth
A burning in my heart no force could stay.

I delved into religion but no peace
There amid the dogmas could I find
I peered in the occult but could not cease
The yearning for company of a higher kind.

And so I met the great minds of the day,
Philosophers and teachers of great wealth,
Of wisdom, courtesy, and strangely they
Accepted me, but one who with a subtle stealth

Called my name and I without a doubt
Crossed the seas and finally came to Her
And in that burning moment my soul came out
And met the One my friend had called 'Great Sir'.

In that transcendent hour I was born
Not reborn as the ancient gospels say
But recreated and the past was torn
From me, my soul to seek the upward way.

Now in my eighties I have come to see
That all my life a single destiny
Was but to serve both God and man,
Imbibe Their force as best I can

And grow into the light the Two brought down
To serve the earth and place on her the crown
Of supernatural beauty that we may see
The eradication of evil's ignominy.

Uninvited Entities

These uninvited entities who come
Interfering with the spirit's need for calm
Into the unsuspecting mind's domain
Bringing their insidious messages,
Vital disturbances, anathema to life
And the body's repetition of its pain
Lay waste the evolving self's upward climb.

The soul weeps and the psychic tears
Do not abate, too great the wasted years
To formulate the future's steps and fears
Abound and deep within the pain seers

Unless a Grace should lift the fallen soul
And enveloping it prevent the drastic fall.

Yagna Shastri

I knew a man who so loved trees
His eyes would tear and he would weep;
The slightest breeze that moved the leaves
Would wake him from his night's deep sleep.

To look again at Beauty's face
And with the trees their bark would feel
The breath and nurturing of Grace
That even broken hearts would heal.

I would walk with him the early morn
And share his joy and his delight
Nothing was out of place, outworn
To mar his visionary sight.

He is gone now this wise Shastri
Friend of earth and friend to me.

In Savitri

In Savitri the world will find its way
Through mantras of magnificence and might
Separation of night from eternal day
To open for us the eye of spiritual sight.

Man who longs for beauty and truth shall find
Apparent to all, even the 'mind impaired'
Or the rational thinker in his well-built blind
The truth Divinity has often aired,

The soul's delight at finding the secret of love
And Death's destruction through its latent power
To heal the pangs of earth by Grace from above
And bring the aspirant psychic being to flower.

In the Home of the Gods

Here in the home of the Gods my soul does dwell
In the Ashram and Auroville old friends I greet
But the violence of the few is hard to quell
In certain beings whose power-lust I meet.

When ego takes possession as the lord
Of the human household and vanity of lust
Failing the wisdom of the eternal word
Lacking the element of mortal trust

The edifice of harmony begins to fall
And all the aspiration of the past
Centuries collapses and the call
Is heard no longer and a spell is cast

Upon the devotees who have come to unite.
May the anger end and evil's strangling blight.

Melodies of Love

Not only did I meet Her in that place
That had no walls but with inner eyes did see
The mystery and marvel of a face
I knew before in Time's eternity.

She spoke to me in tones of liquid gold
Of music that was new on earth and pure
And of the music of the past She told
Of the great composers of the human race,

The chosen ones who captured music's strain
From subtle worlds and spheres above our own,
And often in their illness and their pain
Brought down to earth the songs the Gods had sown

Among the stars, the melodies of love,
These sonic gems from higher worlds above.

Moments

There are moments when we delve deep within
And see ourselves, our lives with different eyes,
A place where neither morality or sin
Can enter the holy realms of Paradise.

I have known love as a sacrament of peace
And in those years opened the psychic gate
Gaining a little in finding a release
From bondage and the pressing karmic fate.

Yet now I am aware of sorrow's core
And not yet free from stains of calumny
Though stronger still than I was before,
In the vital years of love's discovery.

My Love for Thee

I invoke the peace to settle in the mind,
In the stilling of the heart to open up,
Above the head the higher knowledge find
And the nectar divine drink from a cup

Of bliss or a tankard of delight;
To show in every soul a love divine
And with the blessing of the inner sight
Become to all the symbol and the sign

Of a transitional soul born on earth
Who has come in service to the Lord.
Let there be in me no lingering dearth
Of vain resistance before the feet of God,

May all my years on earth be those of praise
And may my love for Thee fill all my days.

New and Glorious Home

When will India in truth be free
Of caste distinctions and unite the race
And with the readiness and alacrity
Approach the dawning world with a new face.

There is in this land a spiritual fire
That can ignite the nations of the world
To turn from itinerant and temporal desire
That the Mother's flag might be unfurled

And the spirit of truth and harmony abide.
Through centuries of the tapas of the soul
Choosing not indolence or in the dark to hide
The Vedic mystics elected to find the All.

Now the Mother and the Lord have come
Announcing the new and glorious home.

On the Shore of Bengal's Sea

Standing on the shore of Bengal's sea,
Breathing the air of Ashram's harmony
I look upon the years that have flown by
Since first I came upon this shore and I
By some unexpected Grace met the Queen,
The Mother of all these souls who have heard the call
From India and far off lands that all
Are welcome to adventure deep within,
Foregoing ritual, device and sin,
The song celestial, the path begin
Forsaking the past and all its vanity
To find within the Peace of sanctity.

Preparing for Sleep

I prepare somewhat unconsciously for sleep,
Invoking always the power of the Name
Repeating it again and yet again to keep
Their blessings always on the weak and lame

Yet sleep does not often upon me fall,
The mind too full of waking thought and toil
The day's events, the entities that call
And remembrance of my hands embracing soil,

The flowers greeting me in fragrant day
The awareness of the body and its role
Watching the way the forces of Nature play
With enticing yearnings to disturb the soul.

Yet one day I will sleep again in peace
And in Their arms will find my soul's release.

She Resides in Me

Foundation of my being I have found
In offering to the descending grace,
There is stability in this shifting ground
Of evolution's swiftly moving pace.

An Ashramite am I, Aurovilian too,
The psychic being having found its home
Beneath Her flag of subtle radiant blue.
I live and work and everything is a poem

Of beauty and transcendence and delight,
Of service to the one who filled my heart
With music and with flowers joyous and bright
May I never from Her heavenly goodness part.

I am Her child, She now resides in me
As the ocean's floor embraces all the sea.

Sing Her Praise

I sat in silence looking at the past
Reviewing all the paths that I have trod,
Seeking the One and finding Her at last
In that hour when I came face to face with God.

She is in me now, no more the need to roam,
The way now found the challenge has begun
Knowing She is seated in this home
Of clay to allow the soul to leap and run

Into Her arms, to kneel before Her Feet,
And look into Divinity's eyes and know
All the striving of this soul is now complete,
And to no higher sphere one need go

But work for Her all present and future days
And softly shall my soul sing her praise.

The Errors of the Past

There are worlds to conquer the epic poet writes,
Worlds of beauty lying deep within
And realms of treachery in those dark nights
When we align with error, falsehood and sin.

Are we now upon the cusp of a new dream
Of unity among the race of men
When all the darknesses in our hearts that seem
To deny the Light that comes to us again

To wash away the errors of the past.
Can we collectively in peace arise
And join in perfect harmony at last
Or shall we linger in the doubt that denies

The Truth that leans towards the aspiring heart
And standing back from Light this life depart.

The Godhead's Face

I live now more aware of the hand of Grace
Touching all the world with Shiva's dance
I bow to those who represent a race
Leaving behind the chains of fate and chance,

Whose souls have opened and the mind subdued
To the thought-streams entering at will
For all the pain and beauty I have viewed
Cannot the longing of my being fill

When there is still such progress to be made,
The emptying of ego and false pride
For all we know is nothing but a shade
Under which our nature tries to hide

From the brilliance of the spirit's view,
The Godhead's face seen only by the few.

The Grace Divine Shall Not Fail

There is an onus on the soul of man
To separate refinement from the rough,
An evolutionary thrust, a span
Through generations of the coarse and tough

Carapace of human desire and need
To survive this lengthy spate of vital unrest
The human condition filled with lust and greed.
Falsehood appears before us as the test

Of mortal sincerity and truthfulness
And though our world is immured in hate and strife
There are sustaining hands and eyes that bless
The sacredness of Nature and human life.

Some preach world's end in cataclysmic hail
But I know the Grace Divine shall not fail.

The Mother's Kiss

What consecration is needed to receive
The light of truth to quell disharmony,
To live in peace no longer forced to grieve
The failing of the light through entropy.

There is a world of bliss awaiting man
If humbly he aspires to forego
Transient joy, the vital's false elan,
Temptations rising daily from below.

A plenary descent has touched our soil,
The promise of a higher life to be
A world of beauty no evil force can foil
A life divine, a home of infinity

And the sweetness of a sanctifying bliss
As we receive on our brows the Mother's kiss.

The Psychic Being Grows

Here I sit clearing the cobwebs of thought
Assigning peace to the turbidness of mind
Which in truth sums up to a single naught
And slowly the calm of soul in me I find.

I shall labour and no gifts of god deny
For am I not in soul and substance free?
The ascent is steep, the summit very high
But ever by my offered self is He.

The centuries pass and the aeons flow
And the psychic being grows upon the way
Yet knowing little I know the path to go
Breaking from the darkest night the day.

The Solace that is Rare

Here now in the turbulent atmosphere
Of the Ashram and in Auroville
Where can one in Covid time, sans fear,
A settled heart and an undaunted will,

Necessity of a developed inner peace,
An unflinching aspiration for the goal,
Surrender fixed, a call that does not cease
Patient like a diamond wrought from coal.

Within the Matrimandir's sacred place
Or standing beneath the steady Service Tree
Who offers shade to the seeking human race
Its branches filled with deep serenity,

This is where the fearless seeker finds
The solace that is rare in mortal minds.

The Spirit's Upward Course

Here on this earth I have set my feet
Crossing vast seas to India my home,
The Mother, Divine, my longing soul to meet
In an Ashram by the Bay of Bengal I come.

In moments when I remember Her I weep
For joy, the heart is filled with gratitude,
For deep in Her my spirit She does keep
Safe, protected from the vile and rude.

My life was changed in meditation's hour,
Kneeling by Her in a room forever still,
Knowing through Her the soul would surely flower
With increasing aspiration and a will

To never halt this journey to the source
Or veer the spirit from its upward course.

The Supermind

A harrowing sorrow fills the heart of man,
His loneliness outpaces his delight
His frozen masterpieces slay elan
His preference favors not the day but night

All beautiful things he often would destroy
Ancient temples and the sacred shrines
Of ages past, with weaponry would toy,
And on the enemy's defeat he dines.

The hour has come of a transfiguring Grace
The human being we know may not survive,
A greater man shall rise to take his place
Unless this mortal being chooses to live

And wash away the darkness in his soul
Aspiring for the now attainable goal.

The Vaunted Calm

Where is the vaunted calm of which you speak
The radiance of the soul that dwells in you?
Past and present sins within you reek,
The old persists and nothing of the new.

Do you love all as you love your little self?
What dwells within the landscape of your mind?
You are no more than a pitiful little elf,
No representative of a higher kind.

And yet they feel a light and find a peace
Surrounding and enveloping you still
But somewhere in your soul there is a crease
That allows unconscious entry of a will

That holds the darkness in your darkened eyes
And all your knowledge eternal truth denies.

The World in Darkness

How vast the world in darkness seemed to lay
Until I chanced upon a Light that did not die,
A love divine that with my soul did play
And a hand that on my offered breast did lie,

Awakening a thirst within my soul
For something unapproachable and pure,
The aspiration for a single goal
Essential to my life, abundant, sure.

And though I have walked upon the errant ways
With a nature vital, wild, untamed, unbound,
Now offer myself a servant soul with praise
As one who long was lost and now is found.

To Her I surrender all I am or may be,
To Him all gratitude in humility.

Their Clarion Call

The lion roars upon the mountain top
His teeth are gone and all his regal pride.
Once king of this land his prowess now must stop
And the hour of his death he must decide.

The warriors of the soul give their life
And all they brought to man from heights above
Hoping to end the reign of hate and strife
And to the world consign their gifts of love

Implant and leave, for none or some have heard
The truth that from their lips awaken few,
This power of Truth. this power of the Word,
Revealing the unknown brought down the new.

As a force of light they came to replenish all
Who hearkened to Them or followed Their clarion call.

This Body Old Yet Young

It seems this body old yet young is still
A tabernacle of love consigned to Thee.
Of life's desires I have had my fill
And aspire to live Thy slave eternally.

The progress of this outer world is slow,
Humanity immured in vice and sin
But for those of us the falsehood down below
Is where we let our consciousness begin.

How many years of preparation found
Us lying in the dark not knowing why
We turned from light and the eternal sound
Forgetting our descent from eternity.

The hour is upon us and we pray
To no longer shun the brilliance of the day!

Towards Sri Krishna's Call

From the voices of the earth I hear a cry,
A poignant call for peace as war runs on,
Muffled by the violence, devoid
Of harmony and beauty and delight.
And yet what I have seen is also true,
Nobility and truth define the man,
Sacrifice and service pave his way,
Surrender to a light not yet his own
Or hidden by the outer sheath of flesh.
The day of reckoning will be one of joy
When we shall turn towards Sri Krishna's call,
Aspire as the flower to the light,
As the sea returns to union with the land
And earth rejuvenates with marvel hues,
Magnificence and majesty divine.

Your Longing Soul

Do not allow the darker forces in
Or Perversity with her alluring smile
With faith and fortitude the path begin
Prohibit those who whisper using guile

To halt the advance of the warriors of light,
Those who break the barriers of mind.
These tempters who would welcome you to night,
Circean beings of the nether kind.

Open the spirit's doors to truth and love,
Allow the guidance time to work its will,
If patient it can all obstructions move
And with peace and beauty the inner chamber fill.

The voyage is long, sail on to the highest goal
Unite with Them who called your longing soul.

Rosemarie

The body is gone but her soul lives on and on,
All beauty of the earth it shall retain,
The devotion and undying love of one
Who lived alone for her, and when the pain
Of her departure lessens with the years
Will remember laughter and the joy they shared,
Awakenings to greater truths, the fears
They vanquished and the challenges they dared
To find that love could deepen and make whole
Two separate beings joined soul to soul.
Now she has soared beyond our earthbound sight
But casts on us her sweetness and her light.

International Publications

Auroville Architecture
by Franz Fassbender

Auroville Form Style and Design
by Franz Fassbender

Landscapes and Gardens of Auroville
by Franz Fassbender

Inauguration of Auroville
by Franz Fassbender

Auroville in a Nutshell
by Tim Wrey

Death doesn't exist
The Mother on Death, Sri Aurobindo on Rebirth
Compiled by Franz Fassbender

Divine Love
Compiled by Franz Fassbender

Five Dream
by Sri Aurobindo

A Vision
Compiled by Franz Fassbender

Passage to More than India
by Dick Batstone

The Mother on Japan
Compiled by Franz Fassbender

Children of Change: A Spiritual Pilgrimage
by Amrit (Howard Shoji Iriyama)

Memories of Auroville - told by early Aurovilians
by Janet Feran

The Journeying Years
by Dianna Bowler

Auroville Reflected
by Bindu Mohanty

Finding the Psychic Being
by Loretta Shartsis

The Teachings of Flowers
The Life and Work of the Mother of the Sri Aurobindo Ashram
by Loretta Shartsis

The Supramental Transformation
by Loretta Shartsis

**The Mother's Yoga - 1956-1973 (English & French)
Vol. 1, 1956-1967 & Vol. 2, 1968-1973**
by Loretta Shartsis

Antithesis of Yoga
by Jocelyn Janaka

Bougainvilleas PROTECTION
by Narad (Richard Eggenberger), Nilisha Mehta

Crossroad The New Humanity
by Paulette Hadnagy

Die Praxis Des Integralen Yoga
by M. P. Pandit

The Way of the Sunlit Path
by William Sullivan

Wildlife great and small of India's Coromandel
by Tim Wrey

A New Education With A Soul
by Marguerite Smithwhite

Featured Titles

Divine Love

The texts presented in this book are selected from the Mother and Sri Aurobindo.

"Awakened to the meaning of my heart. That to feel love and oneness is to live. And this the magic of our golden change, is all the truth I know or seek, O sage."

Sri Aurobindo, Savitri, Book XII, Epilog

A Vision by the Mother

On 28th May 1958, the Mother recounted a vision she once had of a wonderful Being of Love and Consciousness, emanated from the Supreme Origin and projected directly into the Inconscient so that the creation would gradually awaken to the Supramental Consciousness. The Mother's account of this vision was brought out a first time in November 1906, in the Revue Cosmique, a monthly review published in Paris.

A Dream – Aims and Ideals of Auroville
the Mother on Auroville

50 years of Auroville from 28.02.1968 - 28.02.2018

Today, information about Auroville is abundant. Many people try to make meaning out of Auroville – about its conception, to what direction should we grow towards, and, what are we doing here?

But what was Mother's original Dream and what was her Vision for Auroville back then?

Matrimandir Talks by the Mother

This book presents most of Mother's Matrimandir talks, including how she conceived the idea for this special concentration and meditation building in Auroville.

Memories of Auroville - Told by early Aurovilians

Memories of Auroville is a book about the very early days of Auroville based on interviews made in 1997 with Aurovilians who lived here between 1968 and 1973. The interviews presented in this book are part of a history program for newcomers that I had created with my friend, Philip Melville in 1997. The plan was to divide Auroville's history into different eras and then interview Aurovilians according to their area of knowledge. Our first section would cover the years from 1968 till 1973 when the Mother was still in her physical body.

The Way of the Sunlit Path

May The Way of the Sunlit Path be a convenient guide for activating this ancient truth as a support for a Conscious Evolution.
May it illumine the transformation offered to us in the Integral Yoga.

A Dream Takes Shape (in English, French, Hindi)

A comprehensive brochure on the international township of Auroville in, ranging from its Charter and "Why Auroville?" to the plan of the township, the central Matrimandir, the national pavilions and residences, to working groups, the economy, making visits, how to join, its relationship to the Sri Aurobindo Ashram, and its key role in the future of the world. This brochure endeavours to highlight how The Mother envisioned Auroville from its inception, some of the major achievements realised over the years, and some of the difficulties currently faced in implementing the guidelines which she gave.

Mother on Japan

I had everything to learn in Japan. For four years, from an artistic point of view, I lived from wonder to wonder. And everything in this city, in this country, from beginning to end, gives you the impression of impermanence, of the unexpected, the exceptional... ...everything in this city, in this country, from beginning to end, gives you the impression of impermanence, of the unexpected, the exceptional. You always come to things you did not expect; you want to find them again and they are lost – they have made something else which is equally charming.

Auroville Reflected

On 28 February 1968, on an impoverished plateau on the Coromandel Coast of South India, about 4,000 people from around the world gathered for a most unusual inauguration. Handfuls of soil from the countries of the world were mixed together as a symbol of human unity. Why did Indira Gandhi, the erstwhile Prime Minister of India, support this development for "a city the earth needs?" Why did UNESCO endorse this project? Why does the Dalai Lama continue to be involved in the project? What led anthropologist Margaret Mead to insist that records must be kept of its progress? Why did both historian William Irwin Thompson and United Nations representative Robert Muller note that this social experiment may be a breakthrough for humanity even as critics commented, "it is an impossible dream"?

A House For the Third Millennium

Essays on Matrimandir

Nightwatch at the Matrimandir...
A cosmic spectacle; the black expanse above, the big black crater of Matrimandir's excavation carved deep into the soil. The four pillars - two of which are completed and the other two nearing completion - are four huge ships coming together from the four corners of the earth to meet at this pro propitious spot...

Passage to More than India

This book is a voyage of discovery. In 1959 the author, Dick Batstone, a classically educated bookseller in England, with a Christian background, comes across a life of the great Indian polymath Sri Aurobindo, though a series of apparently fortuitous circumstances. A meeting in Durham, England, leads him to a determination to get to the Sri Aurobindo Ashram in Pondicherry, a former French territory south of Madras.

www.ingramcontent.com/pod-product-compliance
Lightning Source LLC
LaVergne TN
LVHW021304080526
838199LV00090B/6014